THE OFFICIAL wolves ANNUAL 2010

Written By David Instone

A Grange Publication

© 2009. Published by Grange Communications Ltd., Edinburgh, under licence from Wolverhampton Wanderers Football Club. Printed in the EU.

Every effort has been made to ensure the accuracy of information within this publication but the publishers cannot be held responsible for any errors or omissions. Views expressed are those of the author and do not necessarily represent those of the publishers or the football club. All rights reserved.

Photographs © Action Images

ISBN 978-1-906211-93-6

£6.99

CONTENTS

7	Season Review 2008-09
14	Season's Stats
15	Fixtures 2009-10
16	Final Championship Table 2008-09
17	Player Stats and Trivia 2008-09
18	Kevin Foley – Player of the Year
21	Awards Night Highlights
24	It Isn't Our First Time
26	Promotion Parties Past
30	My Favourite Things
31	Puzzle Page Part 1
32	Made In Wolverhampton
35	My Favourite Things
36	Player Profiles
45	Wolves Quiz and Puzzle Page Part 2
47	A Very British Promotion
50	New Signings
56	Happy Away Days
59	Changing Places
61	Quiz and Puzzle Answers

SEASON REVIEW 2008/09

AUGUST

When supporters now say what a brilliant start Wolverhampton Wanderers made to their promotion-winning 2009-10 campaign, that isn't 100 per cent true!

The club's first game of the season was actually looking a bit dodgy when they twice fell behind away to Plymouth in a repeat of Mick McCarthy's first League match as Wolves manager two years earlier. But goals by Michael Kightly and substitute Sam Vokes earned a satisfactory 2-2 draw. Vokes was one of four close-season signings and another, Chris Iwelumo, struck twice in an extra-time Carling Cup victory over Accrington Stanley before the first Championship win came spectacularly at the expense of Sheffield Wednesday. Iwelumo again netting a brace and being joined on the score-sheet by Sylvan Ebanks-Blake and David Edwards. The early signs suggested Wolves wouldn't struggle for goals and a fine 2-0 win at Ipswich was followed by an outstanding performance in a 5-1 home victory over newly-promoted Nottingham Forest that took the team to the top of the table. Kightly this time took the main scoring honours with a couple.

The only down-side came in between with the Carling Cup KO of a weakened side on penalties away to Rotherham. But it had still been a mouth-watering start.

SEPTEMBER

Jason Shackell and George Friend had by now been added to a list of summer signings also including Richard Stearman and David Jones, with the need for squad strength underlined by knee injury suffered at Ipswich by a serious George Elokobi. Many Wolves players were off on their international travels before the League programme resumed with an emphatic win at Charlton, where Vokes stepped off the bench to score twice. Ebanks-Blake also netted and did so again when Andy Keogh hit a second-half midweek winner at home to Crystal Palace. The early pacesetters had won five successive Championship matches and made it six of the best by playing superbly in a 3-1 win at Preston despite having Wayne Hennessey and hat-trick hero Iwelumo sent off late on. Things were looking very good.....A 2-0 home win over Bristol City had supporters checking the record books for Wolves' all-time best run of consecutive victories but the month ended with a warning when Reading dazzled under the Molineux lights in a 3-0 away win in which the in-form Matt Jarvis suffered a serious hamstring injury.

7

OCTOBER

Wolves, having looked so impressive for many weeks, suddenly stumbled. They kicked off October by losing 3-1 at Swansea, who were back playing at this level for the first time in 25 seasons.

And, although they recovered by hitting back from behind to beat Coventry, they performed poorly when losing 5-2 at Norwich and being overtaken at the same time by neighbours Birmingham. Their run of seven wins had been followed by a sequence of three defeats in four games.

Midfielder Carlos Edwards had been signed on loan to replace Jarvis and an improvement soon came. A 3-2 victory at Watford, where David Jones and Michael Gray scored for the first time in the season, was followed by a fortunate midweek home win over Swansea, who were sunk by Ebanks-Blake's eighth and ninth goals.

McCarthy's men were back on top of the table and were about to make their position even stronger.

NOVEMBER

Wolves recorded another success against South Wales opposition when they won 2-1 against Cardiff in front of the live TV cameras in the city where they had thrillingly won the 2003 play-off final. Iwelumo and Ebanks-Blake were the scorers, both early on. Burnley were just starting to emerge as one of the Championship's teams of the season when they lost 2-0 at Molineux to a brace by Kightly, most Wolves fans having their first look that day at on-loan Chelsea starlet Michael Mancienne.

He stayed alongside another England under-21 defender Richard Stearman as the run of wins reached five thanks to the club's first success and first goals at Southampton's St Mary's Stadium. Iwelumo was joined on the score-sheet by Jones and was now Wolves' top marksman, one ahead of Ebanks-Blake.

Carl Ikeme was having a good run in goal in place of Wayne Hennessey in a side captained by local boy Karl Henry and kept a clean sheet in a comfortable home win over Blackpool that featured two more goals by Iwelumo. And the tall striker netted twice more in a 3-1 triumph at Sheffield United on a night of outstanding finishing.

For the second time in the season, Wolves had reeled off seven wins in a row but again that was as far as they could go as Birmingham visited them on the last Saturday of the month and impressed in a draw that was secured by Ebanks-Blake's equaliser.

DECEMBER

Wolves were again live on Saturday TV when they returned to London, where they had become used to getting good results. This time, though, they were sunk by a spectacular QPR winner that flashed past the recalled Hennessey.

An early penalty at home to Derby three days later eased any nerves and gave Ebanks-Blake the first of his two and Wolves the first of their three in a straightforward win. Fellow scorer David Edwards also had three to his name for the season after a game that marked Matt Hill's debut for the club.

Player of the Year Kevin Foley became the 11th player to score for the club in 2008-09 when he sealed a 2-0 success at home to Barnsley and central defender Neill Collins sent the squad and their supporters into Christmas in great heart by following up with a late winner at Doncaster.

But any thoughts that promotion was going to be won easily were halted when an impressive Sheffield United side hit back from another Collins goal to record a deserved Boxing Day Molineux draw. Then Blackpool twice bounced back to hold Wolves in front of the Sky cameras on a freezing night at Bloomfield Road, Ebanks-Blake (penalty) scoring for the 15th time in the season and Matt Jarvis for the first.

Wolves, still well clear at the top with Reading now neck-and-neck alongside Birmingham, had to wait ten days for their first game of 2009 after their FA Cup tie at Blues was frozen off. And it was an unhappy start to the year for them as Preston equalised Ebanks-Blake's early goal and ran out good 3-1 Molineux winners. Mick McCarthy rested a few of his big guns for the Cup trip to St Andrew's but saw Keogh and Vokes deliver in their absence to book a fourth-round home tie with Middlesbrough that brought Vokes another goal, only for the Premier League side to score either side of his fine header.

In between the two ties, Wolves turned out on a foul Saturday night at Bristol City and were dissatisfied by the 2-2 they picked up, goals by Collins and Jarvis having put them 2-0 up. Another wobble seemed to be under-way – a fear confirmed when Collins this time netted at the wrong end to give second-placed Reading a 1-0 midweek win at the Madejski Stadium and reduce Wolves' lead over them to only two points, with Birmingham a further two back.

Some breathing space was established with a 3-1 home victory over Watford thanks to strikes by forward trio Vokes, Ebanks-Blake and Keogh but anxious times still lay ahead.

JANUARY

FEBRUARY

With Michael Mancienne back at Chelsea, Jody Craddock was given the chance to reclaim the centre-half spot and there were more new faces on board following the transfer-window signings of Kyel Reid and Nigel Quashie on loan and Christophe Berra in a permanent deal.

Once more, though, results took a downward turn with Ebanks-Blake's joy at hitting a hat-trick in a midweek home clash with Norwich subdued by the 3-3 draw and more so by his late penalty miss four days later in a defeat at Coventry that fell on McCarthy's 50th birthday.

When Wolves lost by the only goal at Burnley, they had unusually gone three games without a League win and were within the reach of Reading and Birmingham with the chasing duo's games in hand. But those sides were also having trouble collecting points.

Wolves scored first and last in a 2-2 home draw with Cardiff that was hardly convincing and fears grew when struggling Plymouth visited Molineux the following weekend and won. It had been a very poor month.

One win in 11 League games was hardly the form of table-toppers but, as the new month dawned, so Wolves dragged themselves out of their nightmare run and kicked on towards the finishing line.

MARCH

They ground out a midweek win at Crystal Palace thanks to Ebanks-Blake's late penalty and repeated the scoreline with the same player this time scoring early in the follow-up game at Sheffield Wednesday. The 2008 Golden Boot winner was making a strong bid to hang on to his prize.

Back at Molineux, a tedious night against Ipswich ended goalless and even a 2-1 win over Charlton – with Iwelumo finally back on the score-sheet for the first time since late November – was a nervous, less than impressive performance.

Another long international break was approaching and Wolves sent themselves into it in joyful mood with a fourth victory in five games. Kightly's second-half goal did the trick at Nottingham Forest and ended his own long scoring famine. The team's form still wasn't great but the League table was highly promising – and promotion wasn't far away.

APRIL

There was still time for one final wake-up call for McCarthy's Wolves and it came on the ground where they had won impressively in the Cup three months earlier. Lee Carsley's first-half sending-off for a bad tackle on Iwelumo came at 0-0 but it was Birmingham who ran out winners by a couple of goals

Iwelumo's season was over and Wolves' campaign still had the potential for a nervous finish, only for three early goals in the televised Good Friday home game against Southampton to make it plain sailing once more. Vokes started the rush, Craddock's even better header carried it on and David Jones rounded the scoring off with a penalty in Ebanks-Blake's continued absence through injury.
And the job was then as good as done when Wolves made it six points out of six over Easter by scoring twice deep in the second half at Derby through Jarvis and Keogh, the Irishman having also broken the ice in a game of twists and turns.

Although Sheffield United were now between Birmingham and Reading in the table, Wolves needed only to beat QPR at Molineux on the 18th of the month to be sure of promotion. This they did thanks to a cross by the highly consistent Stephen Ward that brought Ebanks-Blake's 25th and final goal of the season. It was party-time!

All that remained was the lifting of the Championship title to go with the main prize and the point Wolves needed to make themselves champions came with a draw in McCarthy's home-town of Barnsley thanks to Reid's first goal for them. On and on the celebrations went.....

MAY

Wolves supporters always expect their favourites to do things the hard way.

To win promotion with two matches to spare was a luxury and meant the final fortnight of the campaign could be savoured as several other clubs jostled for the other Premier League places.

There was a carnival atmosphere for Doncaster's last-afternoon visit to Molineux and Stearman's late bouncing header gave Wolves their 27th win and 90th point as the perfect build-up to the presentation of the silverware on the pitch. It had been a memorable season – one for all their fans to relish after the many near misses in previous years.

SEASON'S STATS

- 2008-09 Milestones
  (Coca-Cola Championship unless stated)

- Highest home attendance: 28,252 v Doncaster on May 3 Lowest home attendance: 9,424 v Accrington (Carling Cup) on August 12

- Highest away attendance: 33,079 v Derby on April 13 Lowest away attendance: 5,404 v Rotherham (Carling Cup) on August 26

- Biggest win: 5-1 v Nottingham Forest on August 30 Biggest defeat: 3-0 v Reading home on September 30, 5-2 v Norwich away on October 21

DEBUTANTS

- Richard Stearman, David Jones, Sam Vokes (as sub), Chris Iwelumo (as sub) v Plymouth away on August 9; Jason Shackell v Crystal Palace home on September 16;

- Carlos Edwards, George Friend v Swansea away on October 4; Michael Mancienne (as sub) v Swansea home on October 28;

- Matt Hill v Derby home on December 9; Kyel Reid v Middlesbrough (FA Cup) home on January 24; Nigel Quashie v Reading away on January 27;

- Christophe Berra v Coventry away on February 7; Marlon Harewood v Birmingham away on April 6; Ashley Hemmings v Barnsley away on April 25

FIXTURES

WOLVERHAMPTON WANDERERS F C
BARCLAYS PREMIER LEAGUE FIXTURES - SEASON 2009/2010

SAT	15	AUG	WEST HAM UNITED	H	
TUE	18	AUG	WIGAN ATHLETIC	A	
SAT	22	AUG	MANCHESTER CITY	A	
WED	26	AUG			CARLING CUP 2
SAT	29	AUG	HULL CITY	H	
SAT	12	SEP	BLACKBURN ROVERS	A	
SAT	19	SEP	FULHAM	H	
WED	23	SEP			CARLING CUP 3
SUN	27	SEP	SUNDERLAND	A	4.00 P.M. LIVE ON TV
SAT	03	OCT	PORTSMOUTH	H	
SAT	17	OCT	EVERTON	A	
SAT	24	OCT	ASTON VILLA	H	12.45 P.M. LIVE ON TV
WED	28	OCT			CARLING CUP 4
SAT	31	OCT	STOKE CITY	A	
SAT	07	NOV	ARSENAL	H	5.30 P.M. LIVE ON TV (FA CUP 1)
SAT	21	NOV	CHELSEA	A	
SUN	29	NOV	BIRMINGHAM CITY	H	12.00 NOON (FA CUP 2)
WED	02	DEC			CARLING CUP 5
SAT	05	DEC	BOLTON WANDERERS	H	
SAT	12	DEC	TOTTENHAM HOTSPUR	A	
TUE	15	DEC	MANCHESTER UNITED	A	
SAT	19	DEC	BURNLEY	H	
SAT	26	DEC	LIVERPOOL	A	
MON	28	DEC	MANCHESTER CITY	H	
SAT	02	JAN			FA CUP 3
WED	06	JAN			CARLING CUP SEMI-FINAL (1)
SAT	09	JAN	WEST HAM UNITED	A	
SAT	16	JAN	WIGAN ATHLETIC	H	
WED	20	JAN			CARLING CUP SEMI-FINAL (2)
SAT	23	JAN			FA CUP 4
TUE	26	JAN	LIVERPOOL	H	
SAT	30	JAN	HULL CITY	A	
SAT	06	FEB	BIRMINGHAM CITY	A	12.00 NOON
TUE	09	FEB	TOTTENHAM HOTSPUR	H	
SAT	13	FEB			FA CUP 5
SAT	20	FEB	CHELSEA	H	
SAT	27	FEB	BOLTON WANDERERS	A	
SUN	28	FEB			CARLING CUP FINAL
SAT	06	MAR	MANCHESTER UNITED	H	FA CUP 6
SAT	13	MAR	BURNLEY	A	
SUN	21	MAR	ASTON VILLA	A	12.00 NOON
SAT	27	MAR	EVERTON	H	
SAT	03	APR	ARSENAL	A	
SUN	11	APR	STOKE CITY	H	12.00 NOON FA CUP SEMI-FINAL
SAT	17	APR	FULHAM	A	
SAT	24	APR	BLACKBURN ROVERS	H	
SAT	01	MAY	PORTSMOUTH	A	
SUN	09	MAY	SUNDERLAND	H	
SAT	15	MAY			F.A. CUP FINAL

FINAL CHAMPIONSHIP TABLE 2008-09

Pos	Name	P	W	D	L	F	A	GD	PTS
1	Wolves	46	27	9	10	80	52	28	90
2	Birmingham	46	23	14	9	54	37	17	83
3	Sheffield Utd	46	22	14	10	64	39	25	80
4	Reading	46	21	14	11	72	40	32	77
5	Burnley	46	21	13	12	72	60	12	76
6	Preston	46	21	11	14	66	54	12	74
7	Cardiff City	46	19	17	10	65	53	12	74
8	Swansea City	46	16	20	10	63	50	13	68
9	Ipswich Town	46	17	15	14	62	53	9	66
10	Bristol City	46	15	16	15	54	54	0	61
11	QPR	46	15	16	15	42	44	-2	61
12	Sheffield Wed	46	16	13	17	51	58	-7	61
13	Watford	46	16	10	20	68	72	-4	58
14	Doncaster	46	17	7	22	42	53	-11	58
15	Crystal Palace	46	15	12	19	52	55	-3	56
16	Blackpool	46	13	17	16	47	58	-11	56
17	Coventry City	46	13	15	18	47	58	-11	54
18	Derby County	46	14	12	20	55	67	-12	54
19	Nottm Forest	46	13	14	19	50	65	-15	53
20	Barnsley	46	13	13	20	45	58	-13	52
21	Plymouth	46	13	12	21	44	57	-13	51
22	Norwich City	46	12	10	24	57	70	-13	46
23	Southampton	46	10	15	21	46	69	-23	45
24	Charlton	46	8	15	23	52	74	-22	39

PLAYER STATS 2008-09

Want to have a permanent record of who did what in Wolves' brilliant 2008-09 promotion season? Look no further! Appearances (Championship only, including substitute outings):

45 – Foley
44 – David Edwards
43 – Henry
42 – Stephen Ward, Keogh
41 – Ebanks-Blake
38 – Kightly
37 – Stearman
36 – Vokes
35 – Hennessey, David Jones
31 – Iwelumo
28 – Jarvis
23 – Collins
17 – Craddock
15 – Berra
13 – Hill
12 – Ikeme, Shackell
10 – Mancienne
8 – Gray, Reid
6 – Friend, Carlos Edwards
5 - Harewood
4 – Elokobi
3 – Quashie
2 – Hemmings
1 – Darren Ward

Goals (Championship only):
25 – Ebanks-Blake
14 – Iwelumo
8 – Kightly
6 – Vokes
5 – Keogh
4 – Collins, David Jones
3 – David Edwards, Jarvis
1 – Foley, Craddock, Gray, Reid, Stearman

Did you know?
Sam Vokes started only four Championship matches in 2008-09 but went on as substitute in 32. Darren Ward played only 26 minutes of Wolves' promotion campaign – as a sub at Ipswich in August. George Elokobi went eight and a half months between his third and fourth League outings, thanks to a serious knee injury picked up at Ipswich in August.

Wolves also benefited from three own goals during the League season – by Nottingham Forest's Wes Morgan at Molineux on August 30, Barnsley's Bobby Hassell at Molineux on December 13 and Cardiff's Demitrios Konstantopoulos on February 22.

Did you know?
Richard Stearman waited until the last minute of the final game, against Doncaster, to score his first goal of the season.

Karl Henry failed to find the net at all in 2008-09, having scored three times the previous season. Wolves had only one 0-0 Championship draw in their promotion campaign but had eight when they finished seventh 12 months earlier.

KEVIN FOLEY
WOLVES PLAYER OF THE YEAR

It takes something special for a full-back to be named as Player of the Year. And, by missing only two of Wolves' Coca-Cola Championship matches since he moved to Molineux, Kevin Foley has certainly delivered beyond the call of duty.

When the Luton-born defender received 51 per cent of the 6,000 supporters' votes for the prestigious award, it was his reward for two years of high consistency. Foley, 25 this November, played 45 of Wolves' 46 League games in 2008-09, missing only the home defeat against Preston in January, when he was briefly sidelined with a hamstring injury.

And, remarkably, the only Championship fixture he had missed the previous season after his signing in August, 2007, was also against Preston – this time at Deepdale in the March, when he remained as an unused substitute.

Foley didn't figure in the opening game of 2007-08 against Watford either, simply because it was a few days later that he was signed by Mick McCarthy. But Wolves fans have seen plenty of him since – and thoroughly enjoyed the experience. Even so, the Republic of Ireland squad member was a picture of modesty when called on stage in front of 750 guests at the gala Player of the Year dinner at the Telford International Centre.

He later said: "I'm gobsmacked to have received the award. I was delighted but also taken aback by it all.

"It's a great honour and one that makes me very proud. It's brilliant but words can't really describe how happy I feel to be recognised by our supporters.

"I would just like to thank my team-mates because, without them around me, I wouldn't have been picking up the award."

Manager McCarthy had previously expressed surprise at how the speedy right-back had been left out of the PFA Championship Team of the Year. England under-21 international Kyle Naughton, of Sheffield United, was chosen ahead of him but the manager said his player had been 'top, top drawer.'

"I would just like to thank my team-mates because, without them around me, I wouldn't have been picking up the award."

And he also told him a new contract offer would be on the way in the summer of Wolves' promotion and title-winning celebrations – the second time Kevin has experienced such joy.

Foley, who scored once in 2008-09 (at home to Barnsley) to go with the beauty he had netted in the previous campaign against Norwich at Molineux, was also part of the Luton team who went up from League One in 2005 and who finished only three rungs below seventh-placed Wolves in the following season's Championship.

"When we won the league at Luton, it was similar to this but not as good because this is a division above and means we are going to the Promised Land," he added. "It's the biggest prize of all."

In among all the excitement, Foley did have some sympathy for his former club. While Wolves were starting to relish the challenge of facing Manchester United, Liverpool and the rest, Luton were coming to terms with relegation from the Football League to the Blue Square Premier – a painful drop brought about by the 30-point penalty they started the season with.

Immediate promotion now for Luton and survival in the top flight for Wolves – that would make this another great season for Kevin Foley.

PLAYER OF THE YEAR
AWARDS NIGHT HIGHLIGHTS

Sylvan Ebanks-Blake may have been beaten to the main Player of the Year award in 2009 – but he still didn't leave Wolves' glittering end-of-season dinner empty-handed.

The outstanding striker was named Players' Player of the Year and so had another accolade to sit alongside his second successive Golden Boot – the cherished prize for finishing as the season's top scorer in Coca-Cola Championship matches.
And he had earlier been named in the PFA Championship Team of the Year along with Molineux team-mates Michael Kightly and Richard Stearman.

Not that Ebanks-Blake was the only striker among the prizes at Wolves, whose star-studded celebration dinner had to be moved to Telford because there wasn't a venue in Wolverhampton big enough to seat everyone who wanted to be present! Sam Vokes walked off with the Young Professional of the Year prize and Andy Keogh was selected as the scorer of the Goal of the Year after smashing in a volley in the thrilling 3-2 win at Derby on Easter Monday.

The other main award saw Scott Malone, a young defender who has been on loan with Wolves' partner club Ujpest, named Academy Player of the Year.

John Reynolds was honoured as Supporter of the Year while Jody Craddock, like Ebanks-Blake, was named as a close contender in the voting for the Supporters' Player of the Year award that went to Kevin Foley.

Also chosen was a 'Champagne Moment' – the home win over QPR in April that confirmed that Wolves were back in the Premier League.

IT ISN'T OUR FIRST TIME

"We're Back!" are words that have been heard a lot around Molineux in recent months with the side's return to the Premier League. But the shout "It's Back!" would also have been appropriate.

For the trophy that Karl Henry and Jody Craddock kissed and raised skywards after the home win over Doncaster in May was the same piece of silverware that the likes of Billy Wright and Eddie Stuart often had their hands on in Wolves' glory years. The prize presented these days to the winners of the Championship is the same one that the club won in 1953-54, 1957-58 and 1958-59 as champions of England when , of course, there was no such thing as the Premier League.

Although the success of Mick McCarthy's squad will be the first taste of title-winning delight for many young supporters, Wolves have often had the knack of finishing first in various tables in the past.

In 1987-88, in fact, they became the first club to have won all four divisions when, under manager Graham Turner, they lifted the Fourth Division title.

A year later, they were crowned Third Division champions, having won Third Division (North) way back in 1923-24, when that division was split into north and south sections to cut down on travelling time for teams.

And the club had twice previously won the same division that they climbed out of so thrillingly a few months ago – first in 1931-32 and then in 1976-77. On each occasion, it was then known as the Second Division.

But it's the Championship trophy – the one that will be Wolves' proud property until the end of the 2009-10 season – that is most fondly recalled by older fans.
Wolves had gone close to winning it several times around the Second World War, notably when they finished runners-up to Arsenal in 1937-38 and Everton in 1938-39 and then needed only a last-day draw at home to Liverpool in 1946-47 to become champions. But Liverpool beat them 2-1 and made off with the honours instead. There was time for another second-place finish (behind Portsmouth in 1949-50) before Wolves captured the title for the first time in 1953-54, beating Albion, of all clubs, into second place.

Billy Wright was captain then and still had the role when the trophy was reclaimed four years later, although he was playing for England on the day they made sure of finishing on top of the pile. Eddie Stuart was his deputy and led the players' celebrations in the old Waterloo Road Stand after the 2-0 victory over Preston at Molineux.

Wright was very much present, though, when Wolves registered the home wins over Luton (5-0) and Leicester (3-0) that made them champions again 12 months later. Although the issue wasn't mathematically resolved until the Leicester game, it is the Luton one that is seen as the title-clincher, so much so that Matt Busby, manager of runners-up Manchester United, sent a telegram of congratulation to Molineux after it.
And what about this? The date of that game was April 18, 1959 – precisely 50 years to the day before Wolves beat QPR last spring to make sure of promotion.

PROMOTION PARTIES PAST

We all know how brilliant it felt when Wolves secured their ticket back to the Premier League after five years away.
Here are a few snippets of information, though, from their previous promotions to the top flight of English football.

When the club went up in 1966-67, with Ronnie Allen as their manager, they ran out for their final home match of the season (a 4-1 win over Norwich) with bouquets of flowers which the players presented to girls and ladies in the 27,931 crowd. Unfortunately, the side – unlike Mick McCarthy's men – couldn't follow up the winning of promotion by becoming champions as well. They were beaten 4-1 at Crystal Palace in their final game and had to be content with finishing runners-up to Coventry.

And there was little time for that Wolves team, who included Mike Bailey (skipper), Derek Dougan, Dave Wagstaffe and Peter Knowles, to celebrate. Like the victorious 2009 squad, they headed for America but 42 years ago it was to play for a month and a half in a summer tournament which they won playing under the name of Los Angeles Wolves.

Wolves won promotion from Second Division again in 1976-77, this time at the first attempt. And, in doing so, they helped Nottingham Forest become League champions and then double European Cup winners!

Sammy Chung's side had already assured themselves of the title when they went to Bolton on the last day of the season. The home team, including Dudley-born Sam Allardyce as their centre-half, could still go up themselves but were beaten 1-0 by Kenny Hibbitt's goal – a result that meant Forest finished third instead and went up (there were no play-offs then) behind runners-up Chelsea. A year later, Forest won the top division as well and then won the European Cup (the original name of the Champions League) in each of the following two years, so their manager Brian Clough always had a soft spot for Molineux!
Moving on, Andy Gray, now the no 1 co-commentator on Sky, scored ten goals when Wolves, with Graham Hawkins as manager, went up from the Second Division behind QPR in 1982-83.

And Keith Downing celebrated the winning of the Third Division in 1988-89 by running out for the game at Preston the following Saturday in a blond wig! Wolves had an open-top bus tour shortly afterwards but their two star players, Steve Bull and Andy Mutch, weren't on it. They were away on an England B tour of Switzerland, Norway and Iceland.

The duo had been given the chance to be acclaimed by tens of thousands of fans the year before, though, when a team who had won the Sherpa Van Trophy as well as the Fourth Division title toured Wolverhampton's streets on a chilly Whitsun Monday afternoon.

The only time Wolves have ever been promoted via the play-offs was in 2002-03 when first-half goals by Mark Kennedy, Nathan Blake and Kenny Miller sealed a 3-0 win at Cardiff's Millennium Stadium over Sheffield United, who included former Molineux midfielder Mark Rankine in their midfield.

MY FAVOURITE THINGS

DAVID JONES

Other team: Manchester United
Player: Lionel Messi
Holiday destination: USA
TV programme: Entourage
Band/singer: Michael Jackson

DAVID EDWARDS

Other team: Newcastle United
Player: Paul Gascoigne
Holiday destination: Cancun
TV programme: Only Fools and Horses
Band/singer: Jay-Z

SAM VOKES

Other team: Southampton
Player: Matt Le Tissier
Holiday destination: Dubai
TV programme: The Simpsons
Band/singer: Kings of Leon

CAN YOU UNRAVEL THE WORDS AND NAMES BELOW TO COME UP WITH FIVE PLAYERS WHO HAVE REPRESENTED WOLVES IN 2009? PLEASE IGNORE THE PUNCTUATION, CAPITAL LETTERS AND DODGY SPELLING!

1. Brrr! Cheat Sophie
2. I end free grog
3. J and S Video
4. I heard St Marnarc
5. Tall Tim H.

SPOT THE BALL

LOOK CAREFULLY AT THE PICTURE BELOW AND USING YOUR SKILL, TRY TO WORK OUT WHERE THE BALL MIGHT BE.

Answers on Page 61

MADE IN WOLVERHAMPTON

What do David Beckham, Steve Gerrard, Alan Shearer and Karl Henry have in common?

Answer: They have all captained the clubs they supported as youngsters.

So, imagine the pride you would feel at leading Wolverhampton Wanderers out for a big Premier League fixture - and you start to appreciate the satisfaction Karl has had in captaining his home-city club, not only match-by-match but also for large parts of 2009.

The thrill Beckham would have had pulling on Manchester United's armband, Gerrard has in leading Liverpool to success or Shearer might have felt in years gone by when skippering (rather than managing) Newcastle has been matched at Molineux with Henry at the head of a team who moved up a division after taking the Championship by storm.

"It was a dream come true when Wolves came in for me three years ago," said Henry, who frequently took the arm-band in the club's Championship-winning campaign in the absence of centre-half Jody Craddock. "Being a local lad from a family who all support the club meant it was just brilliant when I moved here as a player.

"So you can probably work out how I felt when we won promotion. None of us will ever forget the elation of beating QPR in front of our own fans to make sure of going up.

"It was the proudest moment of my career without a doubt, 100 per cent. I was captain for the majority of the season and it was a fantastic campaign and fantastic end to it.

"It really was a memorable few weeks but there's never long to dwell on your achievements in football. We knew there was a bigger challenge facing us in the Premier League, so we soon had to get our heads up and be ready to go again."

Henry, who is from the Wednesfield area, is now into his fourth season as a Wolves player, having been transferred from Stoke in Mick McCarthy's first few weeks in charge.

And he has proved himself to be just the sort of young and hungry character the manager loves to have in his side.

He played well-over 30 League games in his first season in the West Midlands and was almost an ever-present until suffering a freak injury - a bruised spleen - soon after scoring the decisive goal in Wolves' 3-2 win at Luton at the start of March.

He was back early the following season, though, and then in 2008-09 missed only three Championship games as promotion was secured in April.

With Stoke easily surviving their first year in the Premier League, there were two obvious fixtures for Henry to look out for this season with extra excitement.

But, with the likes of Manchester United, Liverpool, Chelsea and Arsenal all featuring in Wolves' programme in 2009-10, it isn't hard to pick out highlights!

"The club have been working hard for quite a long time to get here and it's all about trying to make sure we stay up and build from there," the player added.

"A few other teams before us have shown how it can be done and we hope to prove to our fans that we can compete at this level as well.

"We've all been excited about being up here but it will mean a lot more if we can keep our heads above water in the first season."

So when your mood goes up and down depending on Wolves' results, you can be sure that Karl Henry, as a fellow supporter, is feeling just the same.

MY FAVOURITE THINGS

MATT JARVIS

Other team: Manchester United
Player: Ryan Giggs
Holiday destination: Skiathos
TV programme: The Mentalist
Band/singer: Michael Jackson

RICHARD STEARMAN

Other team: Leicester City
Player: Rio Ferdinand
Holiday destination: Dubai
TV programme: Entourage
Band/singer: Ne-Yo

CHRISTOPHE BERRA

Other team: Hearts
Player: Marcel Desailly
Holiday destination: USA
TV programme: Lost
Band/singer: P. Diddy

PLAYER PROFILES

CHRISTOPHE BERRA
Position: Defender
Born: Edinburgh, 31/1/85
Signed: February, 2009
Other club: Hearts

Christophe Berra: Scottish international central defender who Mick McCarthy had trailed for months before his arrival in last winter's transfer window. Has played in Europe and holds a Scottish Cup winners' medal.

NEILL COLLINS
Position: Defender
Born: Irvine, Scotland, 2/9/83
Signed: November, 2006 (initially on loan)
Other clubs: Queens Park, Dumbarton, Sunderland, Hartlepool (loan), Sheffield United (loan)

Neill Collins: Central defender or right-back who has come up with more than his fair share of important goals for Wolves. Well liked by Mick McCarthy for his attitude and determination.

JODY CRADDOCK
Position: Defender
Born: Redditch, 25/7/75
Signed: July, 2003
Other clubs: Cambridge United, Sunderland, Sheffield United (loan), Stoke (loan)

Jody Craddock: Delighted to sign a new contract in the summer after again proving his worth to the club in the promotion campaign. Has considerable captaincy experience and keeps on bouncing back!

SYLVAN EBANKS-BLAKE
Position: Forward
Born: Cambridge, 29/3/86
Signed: January, 2008
Other clubs: Manchester United, Royal Antwerp (loan), Plymouth

Sylvan Ebanks-Blake: Winner of the Championship's Golden Boot last season for the second year running and a terrific finisher. It was no surprise that he should score the goal against QPR that secured promotion.

DAVID EDWARDS
Position: Midfielder
Born: Shrewsbury, 3/2/86
Signed: January, 2008
Other clubs: Shrewsbury, Luton

David Edwards: Welsh international midfielder who has been a steady performer for the club and featured in more than 40 Championship games in 2008/09. A close friend of England under-21 keeper Joe Hart.

GEORGE ELOKOBI
Position: Defender
Born: Cameroon, 31/1/86
Signed: January, 2008
Other clubs: Colchester, Chester (loan)

George Elokobi: Popular left-back who made a surprise return on the last day of last season after being out for nine months with a cruciate knee ligament injury. Hoping to make a good Premier League impact.

KEVIN FOLEY
Position: Defender
Born: Luton, 1/11/84
Signed: August, 2007
Other club: Luton

Kevin Foley: Last season's Player of the Year – Mr Consistency in the eyes of many Wolves fans. His career has gone from strength to strength and finally led him into the Republic of Ireland's senior team.

GEORGE FRIEND
Position: Utility man
Born: Barnstaple, 19/10/87
Signed: September, 2008
Other club: Exeter

George Friend: Has had to be very patient in waiting for his first-team opportunities since arriving at Molineux more than a year ago from one of the clubs in his native Devon.

WAYNE HENNESSEY
Position: Goalkeeper
Born: Anglesey, 24/1/87
Signed: April, 2005
Other clubs: Bristol City (loan), Stockport (loan)

Wayne Hennessey: Now has two virtually full seasons behind him in the first team but has Marcus Hahnemann as competition as well as Matt Murray and Carl Ikeme this term. Well established as a Welsh international.

KARL HENRY
Position: Midfielder
Born: Wolverhampton, 26/11/82
Signed: August, 2006
Other clubs: Stoke, Cheltenham (loan)

Karl Henry: Another man to have led Wolves out on many occasions since his arrival more than three years ago. With his 100 per cent commitment and loyalty, typifies the attitude Mick McCarthy looks for.

MATT HILL
Position: Defender
Born: Bristol, 26/3/81
Signed: September, 2008
Other clubs: Bristol City, Preston

Matt Hill: Fitted in soundly when used in the promotion season after becoming yet another recruit by Mick McCarthy from a smaller club. Thrilled to have the chance to challenge for a place in a Premier League team.

CARL IKEME
Position: Goalkeeper
Born: Sutton Coldfield, 8/6/86
Signed: July, 2003

Other club: Accrington (loan), Stockport (loan)
Carl Ikeme: Much is expected from this tall young keeper, who was born across the West Midlands in an area more known for containing Villa and Birmingham fans! Hoping for a long injury-free run.

CHRIS IWELUMO
Position: Forward
Born: Coatbridge, 1/8/78
Signed: July, 2008
Other clubs: St Mirren, Aarhus, Preston, Stoke, York (loan), Cheltenham (loan), Brighton (loan), Alemania, Colchester, Charlton

Chris Iwelumo: Helped set up the charge for a Premier League place with a sizzling scoring burst in the first half of last season. Went off the boil later and absent for the last month after a nasty injury at Birmingham.

MATT JARVIS
Position: Midfielder
Born: Middlesbrough, 22/5/86
Signed: June, 2007
Other clubs: Millwall, Gillingham

Matt Jarvis: Overcame injury problems to give Wolves real threat on the left wing in the Championship to balance what Michael Kightly gave them on the right. Comes from a talented sporting family.

DAVID JONES
Position: Midfielder
Born: Southport, 4/11/84
Signed: June, 2008
Other clubs: Manchester United, Preston (loan), NEC Nijmegen (loan), Derby

David Jones: Like Sylvan Ebanks-Blake, learned his football at Manchester United. Was a promotion winner at Derby before Molineux but hoping his stay in the Premier League is much longer this time.

ANDY KEOGH
Position: Forward
Born: Dublin, 16/5/86
Signed: January, 2007
Other clubs: Leeds, Bury (loan), Scunthorpe

Andy Keogh: The Republic of Ireland international ended the promotion season on a high after winning over many of the fans who were doubting him. Another who is having his first taste of the Premier League.

MICHAEL KIGHTLY
Position: Midfielder
Born: Basildon, 24/1/86
Signed: November, 2006 (initially on loan)
Other clubs: Southend, Farnborough (loan), Grays Athletic

Michael Kightly: Is often held up as the best of Mick McCarthy's Wolves signings as he was spotted in non-League and later linked with a move from Molineux to Old Trafford! Injury sadly shortened his England under-21 career.

MATT MURRAY
Position: Goalkeeper
Born: Solihull, 2/5/81
Signed: August, 1997
Other clubs: Tranmere (loan), Slough (loan), Kingstonian (loan)

Matt Murray: Has been desperately unlucky with injuries after being tipped by many to become an England international. This real gentle giant deserves much better and hopefully will have good luck in the top flight.

RICHARD STEARMAN
Position: Defender
Born: Wolverhampton, 19/8/87
Signed: June, 2008
Other club: Leicester

Richard Stearman: Soon went from Wolves' promotion celebrations to duty with England in the European Under-21 Championship finals in Sweden. Wolverhampton-born and tipped for a big future.

STEPHEN WARD
Position: Utility Man
Born: Dublin, 20/8/85
Signed: January, 2007
Other club: Bohemians

Stephen Ward: Another player who sums up the 'young and hungry' feeling Wolves thought was needed to get them out of the Championship. Started as a forward at Molineux, now mainly seen as a defender.

SAM VOKES

Position: Forward
Born: Lymington, 21/10/89
Signed: May, 2008
Other club: Bournemouth

Sam Vokes: Scored a vital goal at Plymouth on his Wolves debut and, although not prolific, continued to net through the season – including one v Middlesbrough in the FA Cup and another v Southampton at Easter.

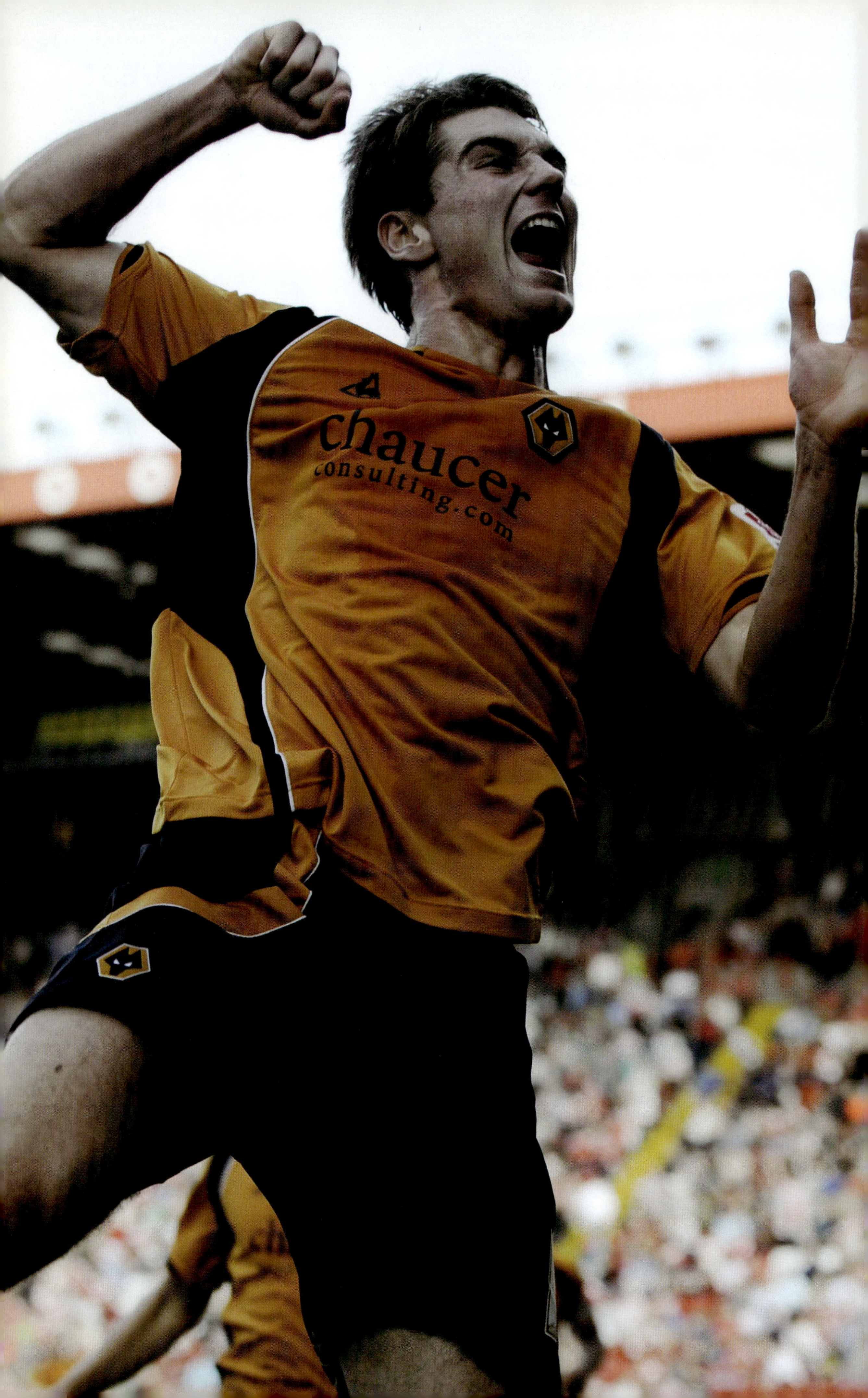
chaucer
consulting.com

HOW WELL DO YOU KNOW YOUR WOLVES?

TEN QUESTIONS TO TEST YOUR KNOWLEDGE ON EVERYTHING TO DO WITH MOLINEUX:

1. Who scored Wolves' last League goal of 2008-09?
2. Who played more Championship games than anybody else for the club last season?
3. Which defender did Wolves loan from Chelsea from late October?
4. Which of these players was NOT sent off in the 2008-09 Championship campaign? Wayne Hennessey, Carl Ikeme, Chris Iwelumo.
5. Which was the only side against whom Wolves scored five goals in a match in their latest promotion season?
6. Who did Wolves beat in the Carling Cup in August, 2008?
7. Which of these games was NOT live on TV last season? Plymouth v Wolves, Cardiff v Wolves, Bristol City v Wolves.
8. True or false? Sylvan Ebanks-Blake scored a hat-trick against Preston.
9. Did Wolves miss a penalty away to Birmingham or Coventry in 2008-09?
10. Which club did Wolves face twice in October last season?

ANSWERS ON PAGE 61

CAN YOU UNRAVEL THE WORDS AND NAMES BELOW TO COME UP WITH THE NAMES OF FIVE FURTHER PLAYERS WHO HAVE REPRESENTED WOLVES IN 2009? AGAIN, DON'T TAKE MUCH NOTICE OF THE PUNCTUATION, CAPITAL LETTERS AND IFFY SPELLING!

Smok Vase
Wii Chum Loser
Kefy in Love
Car Doc Jydd ok?
DDDD airwaves

ANSWERS ON PAGE 61

46

A VERY BRITISH PROMOTION

Not only did Mick McCarthy lead Wolverhampton Wanderers to promotion with a young, hungry squad – he did it with a young, hungry British squad. Look down the squad lists of other clubs on the Internet or on the back page of the programmes in your collection and you will see how many foreign players most of them have.

Wolves have had their fair share of them down the years as well – do you remember Henri Camara, Seol Ki-Hyeon and Seyi Olofinjana, for example, from when and just after they were last in the Premier League?

But the club regained their place in the top flight last spring by relying almost totally on players who qualify to play for the home countries.

"I decided quite early on after joining Wolves that the players I knew best were those who were based with clubs in this country," McCarthy said. "I just thought they were the sort that gave us the best chance of promotion.

"Although I have worked as an international manager with the Republic of Ireland, I didn't feel I knew enough about the level of foreign players who would help us to do well in the Championship."

Mick did say last season, though, that things might be different if and when Wolves were in the Premier League, so we'll all be watching with interest again when the transfer window opens in January.

Of the 35 players the manager used in Championship and cup games in 2008-09, only a couple – Carlos Edwards and George Elokobi – are able to appear in international football for teams outside the British Isles and Republic of Ireland.

And Edwards, who plays for Trinidad and Tobago, was signed on loan from Sunderland while Elokobi, whose parents are from the Cameroon in Africa, was bought from Colchester, so both of those were well known in this country. Looking back over McCarthy's three-and-a-bit years in charge at Molineux, the pattern is the same. He has signed 40-odd players for the club and they are virtually all regarded as British.

You need to have a good memory or excellent football knowledge to know the odd ones out. The other foreigners he has signed are Danish goalkeeper Jan Budtz (on loan in 2007), Brazilian Gui Finkler (on loan in 2006 but didn't play a single competitive game for the club) and American forward Jemal Johnson (in 2006). Maybe Mick's buying policy is partly because he is so proud of his roots.

The manager, who celebrated his 50th birthday during the second half of last season, was delighted when Wolves clinched the Championship title with their draw at Barnsley. He was born in the Yorkshire town and won the first two of his promotions as a player when he was playing as a tough central defender for them.

When he went up to the top flight with Manchester City in 1985, it meant he had won promotions from all of the three divisions it is possible to do so. And, after including a League and Cup double among his successes in Scottish football with Celtic and having a spell in France with Lyon, he turned his attention to management, at first with Millwall.

He later had six years in charge of the Republic of Ireland before returning to club football and helping Sunderland into the Premier League as champions – as he did with Wolves four years later.

49

NEW SIGNINGS

NAME: NENAD MILIJAS
BORN: BELGRADE, 30/04/83
POSITION: MIDFIELDER
SIGNED: JUNE, 2009
PREVIOUS CLUBS: ZEMUN, RED STAR BELGRADE

Wolves were delighted to complete the signing of this 6ft 2in central midfielder, who has twice won the Serbian league and cup with Red Star Belgrade.

Milijas signed a four-year deal as the club's first signing after the winning of promotion and joined up with his new team-mates on their trip to Australia in July.

He has experience of being a captain with Red Star and was also their top scorer with 18 goals last season.

That total, combined with his all-round play, was enough to make him the Serbian Superliga Player of the Year for 2008-09 and earn him a four-year contract at Molineux.

When he arrived in England for the first time, he already had a double-figure number of caps for his country and now hopes his Premier League experiences will further enhance his reputation.

"I want to help Wolves and I am sure they will help me in my career as well," he said. "For me, the Premier League is the best and hardest league in the world.

"It has been my ambition to play there for a long time."

NAME: MARCUS HAHNEMANN
BORN: SEATTLE, 15/06/72
POSITION: GOALKEEPER
SIGNED: JUNE, 2009
PREVIOUS CLUBS: SEATTLE SOUNDERS, COLORADO RAPIDS, FULHAM, ROCHDALE (LOAN), READING (LOAN), READING

For several seasons, Wolves have had highly talented young goalkeepers. Last summer, Mick McCarthy added a bit more experience to the group. Marcus Hahnemann celebrated his 37th birthday before the club kicked off their second Premier League season but that didn't stop the manager saying he expected him to challenge for a first-team place.

The American, who has more than half a dozen USA caps, spent two seasons in the top flight with Reading, for whom he played almost 300 competitive matches.

"I am excited to be here," Hahnemann said. "My buddy Kasey Keller (who worked with Wolves' manager at Millwall) played with Mick McCarthy and when I told him what was happening, he said it would be great for me to come to Molineux."

The bald last line of defence said the fact that he had enjoyed the atmosphere of Wolves' home as a Reading player was another factor behind his transfer to the West Midlands.

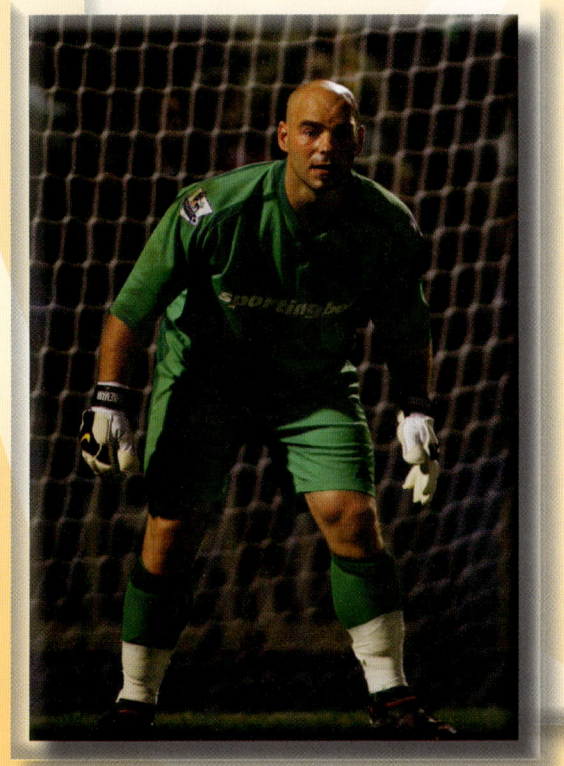

Although he initially signed a deal for only one season, there is an option for a second year if he does well.

And his presence might just help the likes of Wayne Hennessey, Carl Ikeme and Matt Murray to become even better goalkeepers.

NAME: KEVIN DOYLE
BORN: ADAMSTOWN, COUNTY WEXFORD, 18/09/83
POSITION: FORWARD
SIGNED: JUNE, 2009
PREVIOUS CLUBS: CORK CITY, READING

What a coup it was when Wolves beat some established Premier League clubs and made Kevin Doyle their most expensive ever signing.

Mick McCarthy was delighted to lure yet another Irishman to Molineux – this one the highest-profile of them all as he has been a star at Reading for several seasons.

Doyle scored 56 goals in 163 games for the Royals, including 18 in the Championship last season and 13 when they did so well in the Premier League in 2006-07.

He was named as the Football Association of Ireland's Player of the Year in 2008-09 and seemed certain to quickly add to his total of 25 international caps when this season started.

A four-year contract shows how highly Wolves rate him – and the respect of the player for the club is clear as well.

"The facilities here are top-class and it's great for me to be going into the Premier League again," he said. "This is a fresh start.

"Wolves were the first club that actually came in for me, so they were the first club I spoke to. It was nice to see how keen they were."

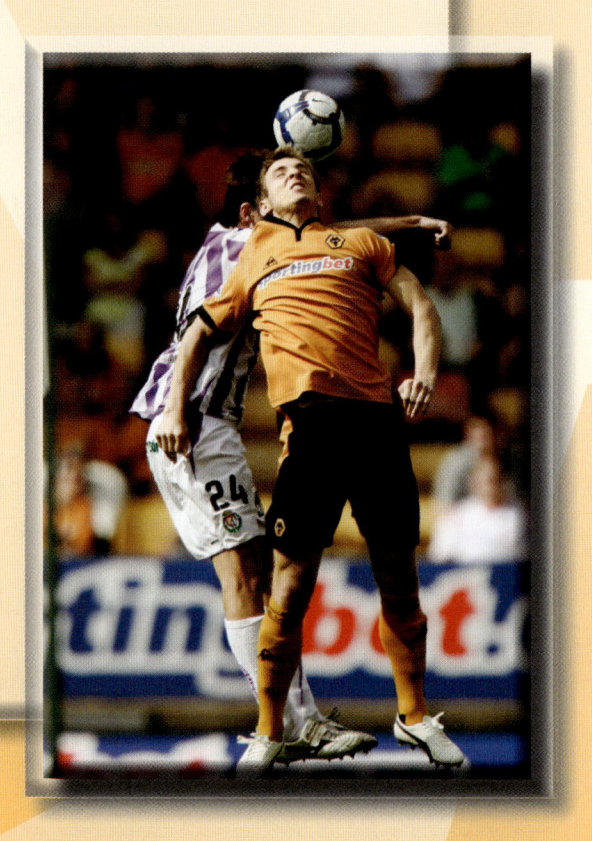

NAME: ANDREW SURMAN
BORN: JOHANNESBURG, 20/08/86
POSITION: MIDFIELDER
SIGNED: JULY, 2009
PREVIOUS CLUBS:
SOUTHAMPTON, WALSALL (LOAN), BOURNEMOUTH (LOAN)

Even before the ink on Kevin Doyle's contract had dried, Wolves swooped back into the transfer market to sign Andrew Surman.

The former England under-21 international moved the following day and offers his new manager plenty of options.

Surman, although often regarded as a left-sided midfielder, can play anywhere across the middle of the field and also at left-back.

Born in South Africa when his father was working there, he played 146 matches for his first club and was disappointed to be relegated with the Saints in May.

He had already had one spell in the West Midlands, though, with Walsall taking him on loan, as Bournemouth also did.

Surman signed a three-year contract and said: "This is a great move for me and I'm really excited to be here.

"To come to a Premier League club and one as big as Wolves is fantastic."

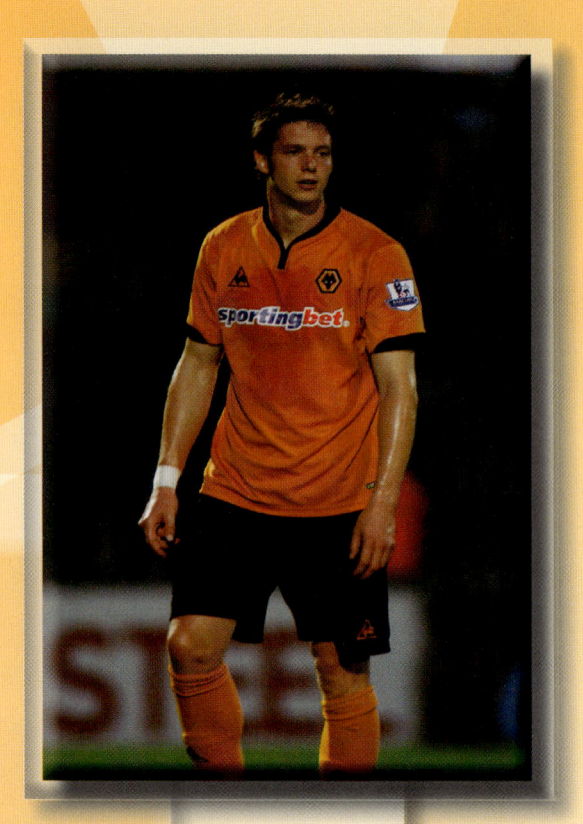

NAME: GREG HALFORD
BORN: CHELMSFORD, 08/12/84
POSITION: UTILITY MAN
SIGNED: JULY, 2009
PREVIOUS CLUBS: COLCHESTER, READING, SUNDERLAND, CHARLTON (LOAN), SHEFFIELD UNITED (LOAN)

Greg Halford became Wolves' third signing in four thrilling days when he arrived at Molineux on a three-year contract just before the squad departed on their pre-season trip to Australia.

Only a few weeks earlier, he had been striving as a loan player to take Sheffield United into the Premier League via the play-off final, having scored the vital goal in the Blades' semi-final victory over Preston.

The defeat against Burnley left him frustrated, though, and he checked back in at his parent club Sunderland before heading south in a permanent deal. "It always plays a big part when a manager shows how much he wants you," Halford said. "Obviously I had also heard a lot of good things about him from other people.

"Trying to prove myself at the top level is another reason for the move." He cost both Reading and Sunderland £2.5m but played only a handful of games for either and was seen much more when on loan, initially to Charlton, where he scored against Wolves in 2007-08.

The right-back or midfielder has also played up front on occasions and is a long-throw specialist.

NAME: RONALD ZUBAR
BORN: GUADELOUPE, 20/09/85
POSITION: DEFENDER
SIGNED: JULY, 2009
PREVIOUS CLUBS: CAEN, MARSEILLE

Mick McCarthy used to be a tough central defender in club and international football, and he saw a similarity with himself in the playing style of his sixth summer signing.

Although Ronald Zubar used to play in midfield and has sometimes been used as a right-back, it is as a centre-half that he is now best known. He was linked with Arsenal and Lyon in the past and played for Marseille against Liverpool home and away last season as part of his considerable Champions League experience.

The former French under-21 international also previously played for Caen, with whom he won promotion and suffered relegation as well as reaching the French League Cup final.

Now, though, he is hoping to make this a good first season in English football as he settles into life on a four-year contract here.

Zubar is hoping to one day play in the French national team despite already having a full international cap for Guadeloupe, a French region in the Caribbean. Because the island is not recognised by FIFA, he is still free to play for another country.

His younger brother is a professional footballer in Romania.

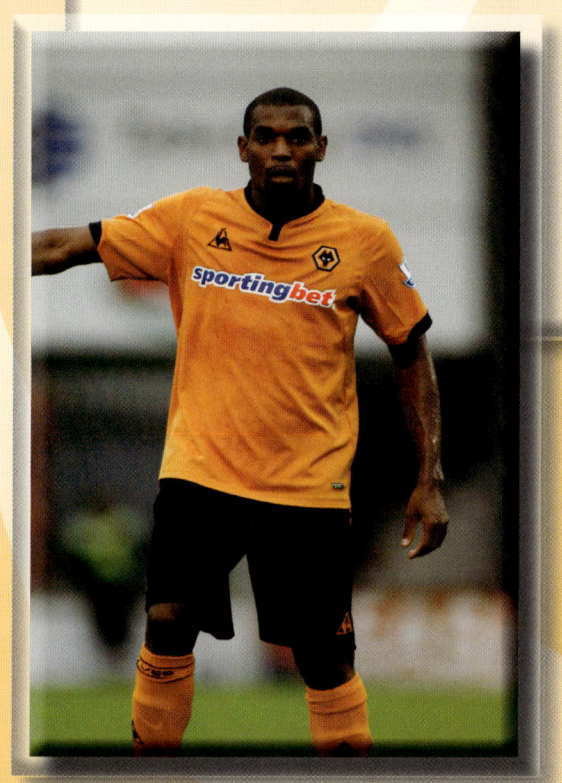

HAPPY AWAY DAYS!

Which was your favourite away game of 2008-09? The win at Birmingham in the FA Cup, the one in the League at Derby over Easter or maybe the draw at Barnsley a couple of weeks later that brought the Championship trophy to Molineux? Whatever your personal choice, you can be thankful that you were a witness to one of the best seasons Wolves have ever had on their travels.

In fact, if they had won at Barnsley in their final trip, they would not only have finished with 92 points – an average of exactly two per game – but would also have equalled the highest number of away League wins in a season in their history. Their 12 Championship successes 'on the road' meant they had two more than any other club in the division (Sheffield United totalled ten) but their tally was one short of when they won 13 in 1958-59.

Not surprisingly, they also gathered a lot of points when they went up and down the country for their games in previous promotion campaigns. They had 11 away League wins under Dave Jones in 2002-03, eight when they became Third Division champions under Graham Turner in 1988-89 and 12 the previous year when the same manager inspired them to the Fourth Division title. But it may seem a little odd that the season in which the club equalled what was then their highest number of away victories in League or cups did not come in one in which they went up. In their 1986-87 Fourth Division campaign, Wolves won 14 times on other clubs' grounds but finished fourth in the table and were then beaten by Aldershot in a two-leg play-off final!

Twelve months later, they set a new club record when winning 15 times away from Molineux – or 16 if you include the Sherpa Van Trophy final at Wembley. And take a look down this list of some of the places where they won around that time and you'll realise how far the club have come......Lincoln, Torquay, Hartlepool, Halifax, Rochdale, Exeter, Hereford and Newport; all of them venues Wolves are unlikely to visit for a long while unless it is in a cup competition or for a friendly. Compare that group of names with some of the famous grounds Wolves won at when they had a then club record 13 away League victories on their way to winning the First Division (now Premier League) title for the third and latest time in 1958-59.......Aston Villa, Portsmouth, Newcastle, Manchester City, Everton.

And, to finish with, what about these spectacular Wolves away wins from their 1949-1960 glory years?

Liverpool 1 Wolves 4 (Dec 16, 1950)
Huddersfield 1 Wolves 7 (Sept 29, 1951)
Manchester United 0 Wolves 3 (Feb 21, 1952)
Manchester City 0 Wolves 4 (Aug 22, 1953)
WBA 0 Wolves 1 (Apr 3, 1954)
Cardiff 1 Wolves 9 (Sep 3, 1955)
Birmingham 1 Wolves 5 (Oct 12, 1957)
Manchester United 0 Wolves 4 (Apr 21, 1958)
Portsmouth 3 Wolves 5 (Dec 26, 1958)
Manchester City 4 Wolves 6 (Sep 5, 1959)
Chelsea 1 Wolves 5 (Apr 30, 1960)

57

58

A lot has happened to the Premier League since Wolves were last in it in 2003-04. The top four places might be filled by the same clubs as they were some five and a half years ago but they finished in a very different order a few months ago when Wolves were putting the final touches to their title-winning triumph.
In 2004, it was Arsenal who were crowned champions at the end of a season in which they were run close at Molineux before pulling away to win 3-1. And they lifted the title by an amazing 11 points!

Manchester United were 15 behind in third spot and fourth-placed Liverpool were all of 30 points off top spot.

Wayne Rooney had still not moved to Old Trafford and was part of the Everton team who Dave Jones's Wolves side beat 2-1 at Molineux just before the end of the season.

Edwin Van Der Saar was playing elsewhere as well and didn't enjoy facing Wolves. The Fulham squad he was then part of were beaten 2-1 on their visit to the West Midlands after the sides drew 0-0 at QPR's Loftus Road, the ground Fulham were sharing at the time while their Craven Cottage stadium was being redeveloped. Theo Walcott had just turned 14 when Wolves beat Sheffield United in the play-off final at the Millennium Stadium in 2003 and Cesc Fabregas was playing only his second Arsenal game when he scored in the victory against Wolves in the Carling Cup in December, 2003. And the Gunners were then playing at their old Highbury home rather than at the sparkling Emirates Stadium.

What else was different? Fernando Torres and Dirk Kuyt hadn't kicked a ball for Liverpool and Chelsea fans hadn't seen anything of Didier Drogba, Michael Ballack or any number of their other overseas stars.

And, more generally, the 20 teams who made up the Premier League in the season leading up to the 2004 European Championship finals in Portugal had what you might now think is a surprise look.

Newcastle finished fifth, Charlton seventh, Middlesbrough 11th and Southampton 12th. Wolves won't be playing any of those four clubs in the League this season, nor will there be points at stake if they face Leeds or Leicester – the two sides who they were relegated with, all three of them level on 33 points.

The six different teams in the top flight this time are Burnley, who haven't played at this level for 33 years, Hull, Stoke, Sunderland, West Ham and Wigan.
This will be the first season in which Wolves have ever played Hull or Wigan in England football's leading division and Mick McCarthy's team will be hoping to repeat at least some of the club's experiences from six years ago.

Did you know, for example, that Wolves beat Manchester United 1-0 at Molineux in the League in a Saturday lunchtime game shown live on TV? They beat Manchester City by the same score and comfortably defeated Leeds and Middlesbrough.
But possibly the most memorable game was the one in the October in which they were losing 3-0 at home to Leicester at half-time – and hit back to win 4-3!

60

ANSWERS

HOW WELL DO YOU KNOW YOUR WOLVES QUIZ (on Page 45):

1. Richard Stearman.
2. Kevin Foley.
3. Michael Mancienne.
4. Carl Ikeme.
5. Nottingham Forest.
6. Accrington Stanley.
7. Plymouth v Wolves.
8. False (it was against Norwich; Chris Iwelumo hit a hat-trick against Preston).
9. Coventry.
10. Swansea City.

ANAGRAMS (Page 31):

1. Christophe Berra.
2. George Friend.
3. David Jones.
4. Richard Stearman.
5. Matt Hill.

ANAGRAMS (page 45):

1. Sam Vokes.
2. Chris Iwelumo.
3. Kevin Foley.
4. Jody Craddock.
5. David Edwards.

SPOT THE BALL (page 31):